STEPHEN HAWKING

GREAT LIVES IN GRAPHICS

Button
BOOKS

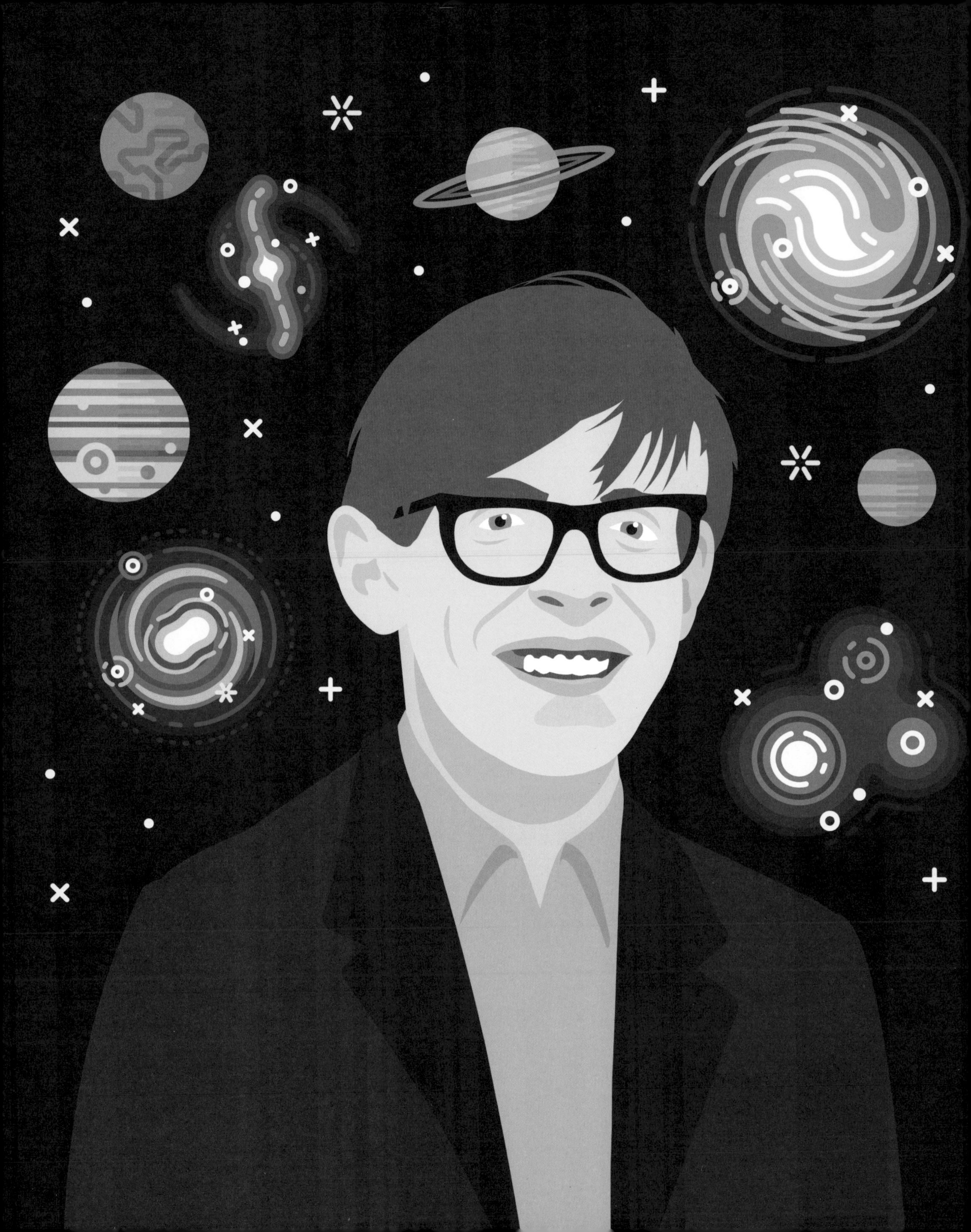

Stephen Hawking is one of the most famous scientists in the world. When he was a child he would look up at the stars and dream about going into space. He never managed it, but his brilliant books about the wonders of the universe brought space a little closer to us. And his bravery and determination to succeed in the face of a disease that left him unable to walk or talk showed everyone what was possible if you never give up.

This is his story–from black holes to bees in the basement to a flight on the "vomit comet," it's filled with incredible achievements, unexpected facts, and surprising adventures. Can you imagine how happy Stephen would have been if it inspired you to change the world, too?

STEPHEN'S WORLD

Born in Oxford, England
1942

1943
Sister Mary born

World War II ends
1945

1947

Sister Philippa born

Family moves to St. Albans
1950

1966
England wins World Cup. Stephen earns PhD

Marries first wife Jane Wilde
1965

1964
Starts using wheel-chair

Diagnosed with ALS. Goes to Cambridge Uni to do PhD
1963

1967
First son Robert born. Beatles release *Sgt Pepper's Lonely Hearts Club Band*

Man walks on moon
1969

1969
Daughter Lucy born

Publishes first book
1973

197

Publishes books nos. 6 & 7
2002

2001
Publishes book no. 5. Twin towers 9/11

Publishes book no. 4
1998

1995
Marries nurse Elaine Mason

Appears o *Star Trek a* himself. Publishes book no. 3

2004
Says has solved black hole paradox

Rides on "vomit comet"
2007

2009
Awarded US Medal of Freedom

Syrian Civil War begins
2011

2012
London Olympi

1951
First color TV in US

1952
Elizabeth II becomes Queen

Joins St. Albans school. Structure of DNA discovered

1953

1955
Martin Luther King Jr. bus boycott

1962
Gets first degree in Natural Sciences

Yuri Gagarin is first man in space

1961

1959
Studies science at Oxford Uni age 17

Britain tests nuclear bomb

1957

1956
Brother Edward adopted

Proves Hawking Radiation. Rubik's Cube invented

Elvis Presley dies

1977

1979
Son Timothy born

IBM launches first PC with Microsoft

1981

1982
Awarded CBE by the Queen

1993

Gulf War begins

1990

1989
World Wide Web invented

1988
Publishes *A Brief History of Time*

Can't talk, uses voice synthesizer

1985

Publishes memoir

2013

2014
Life story in movie *The Theory of Everything*

Begins project to search for alien life

2015

2016
UK votes for Brexit

Dies March 14, age 76

2018

CANADA

Traveled two miles down a mine shaft to visit an underground laboratory

WHITE HOUSE

Awarded Presidential Medal of Freedom by Barack Obama

Spain

CALTECH CALIFORNIA

Worked at leading tech school from 1974 to 1975 and visited for a month almost every year after

Stephen was an adventurer at heart and being in a wheelchair didn't scare him. He spent most of his life living and working in Cambridge in the UK, but he was also an intrepid traveler who never missed an opportunity for a new experience.

Easter Island

OUT OF THIS
WORLD

ANTARCTICA

Labeled this his favorite trip ever–his wheelchair didn't have snow chains, so fellow physicists drove him around on a snowmobile

OXFORD

The city where he was born, earned his degree, and met his wife Jane

CAMBRIDGE

Stephen's home, where he studied for his PhD, wrote *A Brief History of Time,* and taught at the university

CERN GENEVA

Caught pneumonia while visiting and lost ability to speak

Iran

India

South Africa

LONDON

Awarded CBE by the Queen at Buckingham Palace

. . . .

Given starring role in the opening ceremony at London 2012 Paralympic Games

. . . .

Stephen's ashes are buried in the Scientist's Corner, between Isaac Newton and Charles Darwin, at Westminster Abbey

CHINA

Reached cult status in China. Joined its social media platform Weibo in 2016 and amassed millions of followers in hours

HOME SWEET HOME!

Stephen's mom and dad, Frank and Isobel, were both scientists. They lived in London, but during World War II they moved to Oxford to escape the bombing, and Stephen was born there. When he was eight his dad got a new job and the family moved to St. Albans. Stephen grew up here with his little sisters Mary and Philippa, and adopted younger brother Edward. The Hawkings were great thinkers and Stephen says the neighbors thought they were "eccentric."

PHYSICS

Mostly they ate dinner in silence, each of them reading a book

They made fireworks in the garden greenhouse

The family played board games and Stephen made up his own with his friends

Their new home was rundown but nothing ever got fixed because the family didn't have much money

The family car was an old London taxi

As a young boy Stephen loved to climb. He and his sister Mary would try to find new and exciting routes into their house

Stephen's mom would lie in the garden with the children on summer evenings to gaze up at the stars

They liked to keep bees in the basement

LEARNING CURVE

AGE 8

Stephen learns to read. He thinks his sister Philippa is smarter than him because she can read age 4

AGE 9

Stephen is clever, but he isn't top of his class–in fact, at one point he's three from the bottom

His work is messy and his teachers pull their hair out over his handwriting

His classmates think he's pretty brainy though–they nickname him "Einstein"

AGE 11

Stephen starts high school at St. Albans, where he shows a talent for science and math

AGE 13

His dad wants him to go to the private Westminster School, but he can't afford the fees without a scholarship. On the day of the exam Stephen is sick, so he stays at St. Albans

Stephen loves to take radios and clocks apart to see what makes them tick. One day he and his school friends build a computer from an old clock, a telephone switchboard, and other recycled parts

Stephen guesses he spent 1,000 hours studying at Oxford University

When Stephen started school he didn't stand out as a special student. But as the years went on, he realized he had to make the most of the time he had, and he began to shine.

AGE 17

He takes his entrance exam a year early and wins a scholarship to Oxford University

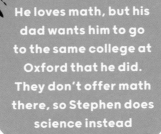

He loves math, but his dad wants him to go to the same college at Oxford that he did. They don't offer math there, so Stephen does science instead

AGE 20

Stephen gets a first-class degree from Oxford despite not doing much work

He goes to Cambridge University to do a PhD in math, physics, and cosmology

DID YOU KNOW?

Stephen only just got his first from Oxford. His score on the exam wasn't quite good enough, so he had to take a spoken exam, too. He was sure his teachers saw him as lazy, so he told them: "If you award me a first, I will go to Cambridge. If I receive a second, I shall stay in Oxford, so I expect you will give me a first." They realized Stephen was probably smarter than any of them and gave him a first

Cosmology is the study of the universe

AGE 24

Becomes the Lucasian Professor of Mathematics at Cambridge University, a top job that only 19 people have had since 1663, including Sir Isaac Newton

AGE 38

He earns his PhD and goes on to win the famous Adams Prize

$715,000
How much a copy of Stephen's PhD essay sold for at auction

ROW, ROW, ROW

When Stephen got to Oxford University he felt bored because he found the work too easy. He looked around for something more exciting and it wasn't long before he discovered rowing. He had a loud voice but a small frame and this made him the perfect "coxswain"–the brains of the boat. Pronounced "cox-en," his job was a bit like that of a coach, helping to steer and encouraging the rowers to go faster.

THE BUFFER

Number 7 links the front and back rowers. He watches number 8 and copies him so that the rest of the boat knows what to do

7

8

6

COXSWAIN

The cox is the smallest of the crew. He steers the boat and yells at the rowers to make them go quicker

THE STROKE

Number 8 is strong but also has great technique–he's in charge of the rhythm. He sets the pace and the rest of the boat follows

800kg

90.00KG

The weight an 8-oared boat can carry

8-oared boats are called "shells"

The boat weighs 90kg

It's 60ft long

THE BOAT

14 mph

The speed the fastest 8-oared boat can reach

55kg

The minimum the cox can weigh (it's 50kg in a women's boat)

1829

The year the first Oxford and Cambridge boat race took place

5

4

3

2

1

ENGINE ROOM

3, 4, 5, and 6 are the big, strong rowers. They don't worry about balance, they just pull as hard as they can

BOW PAIR

Right at the front of the boat, 1 and 2 are brilliant technical rowers who keep the boat balanced in the water

September

4

5

10

rowing pm

1

11

7

rowing pm

16

3

17

8

Spending six afternoons a week rowing meant Stephen missed a lot of his studies

body SHOCK

When Stephen was 21 he started to trip up a lot and act in a clumsy way. He went home for Christmas and his family felt worried and called the doctor. After two weeks of tests they discovered he had a brain disease called ALS that slowly makes your muscles stop working. Most sufferers die within five years, but incredibly Stephen lived until he was 76.

2 YEARS
How long the doctors said Stephen had left to live

55 YEARS
How much longer Stephen lived for

5 out of 100,000
PEOPLE GET ALS AROUND THE WORLD

Only **1 in 4** patients survive longer than five years

Before his illness, Stephen had felt bored with life and didn't always try his best. When he realized he may not have long to live, he started working really hard

> “However difficult life may seem, there is always something you can do, and succeed at. It matters that you don’t just give up”

Stephen Hawking, 2016

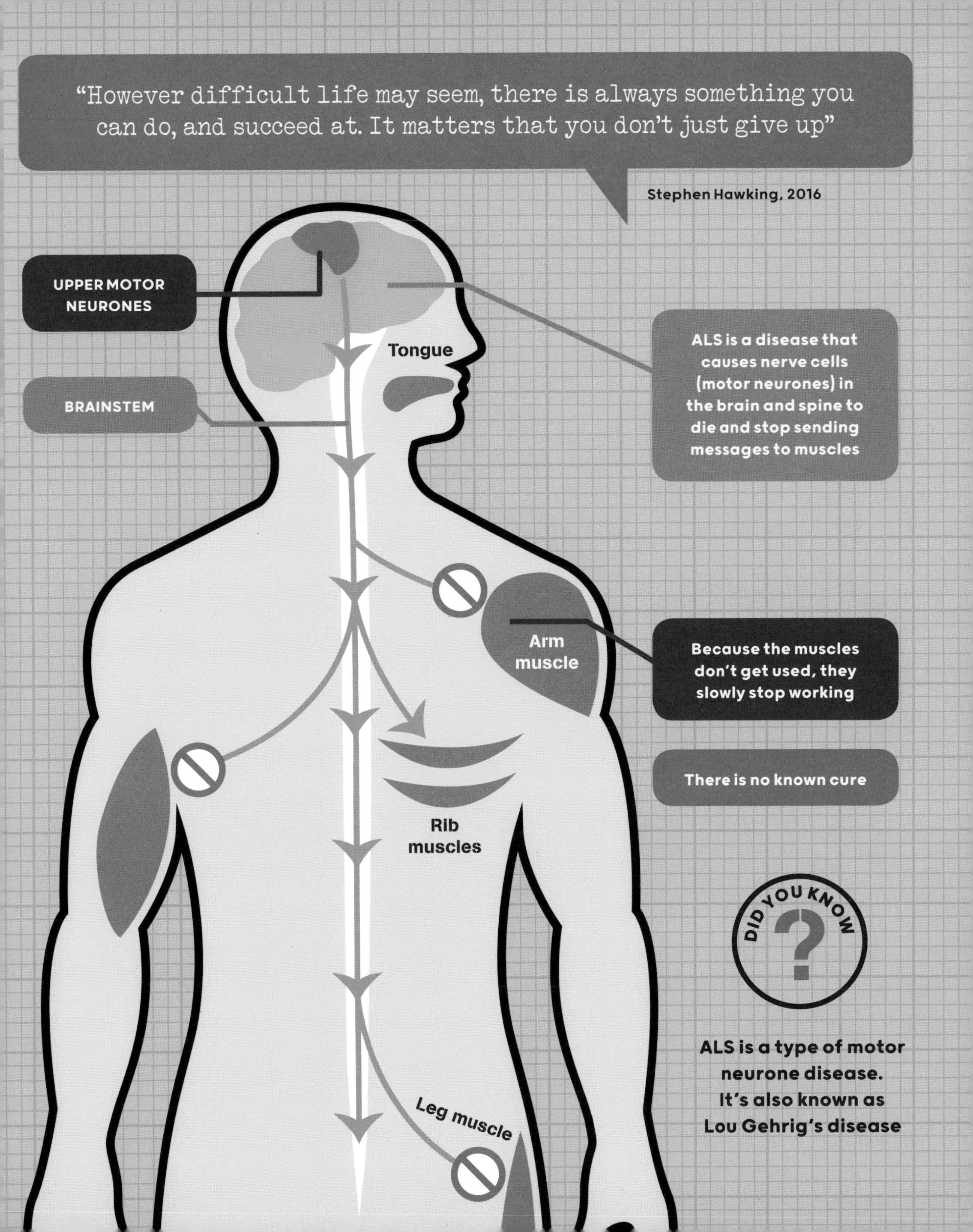

UPPER MOTOR NEURONES
BRAINSTEM
Tongue
Arm muscle
Rib muscles
Leg muscle

ALS is a disease that causes nerve cells (motor neurones) in the brain and spine to die and stop sending messages to muscles

Because the muscles don’t get used, they slowly stop working

There is no known cure

DID YOU KNOW ?

ALS is a type of motor neurone disease. It’s also known as Lou Gehrig’s disease

Dust released into the atmosphere would block out sunlight, causing a long-lasting nuclear winter

20 YEARS

4 MINUTES

How long it would take for a Russian bomb to reach Britain

NUCLEAR CLOUD

In the 1960s, people in Britain had plenty to be worried about. TV programs warned them of the threat of a nuclear attack as countries around the world raced to build nuclear bombs after World War II. Living with the fear that they could be blown away at any moment made people determined to make the most of the time they had. When Stephen was diagnosed with ALS he had just met his future wife, Jane Wilde. When asked why she was willing to marry Stephen despite his disease, she said they wanted "to make the most of whatever gifts were given us."

"I have lived most of my life in the expectation of an early death, so time has always been precious to me. I have so much that I want to do. I hate wasting time"

Stephen Hawking, 2006

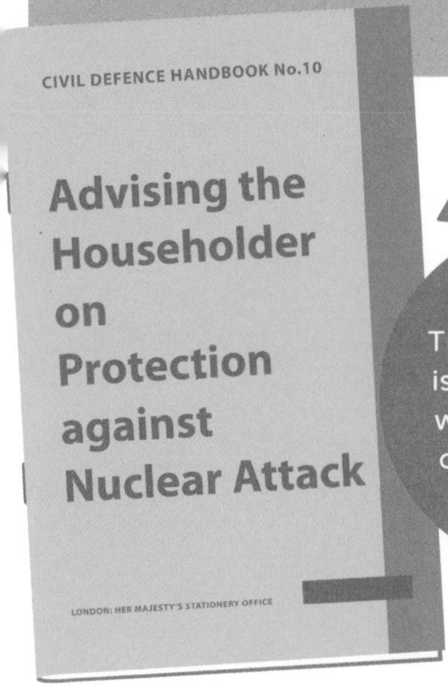

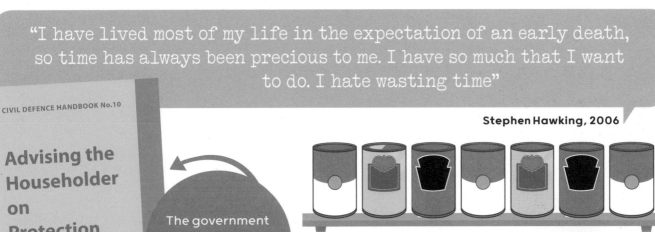

CIVIL DEFENCE HANDBOOK No.10
Advising the Householder on Protection against Nuclear Attack
LONDON: HER MAJESTY'S STATIONERY OFFICE

The government issued everyone with a practical advice booklet

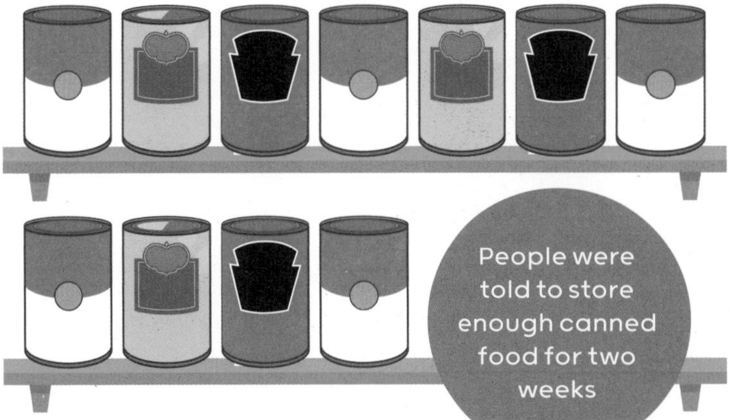

People were told to store enough canned food for two weeks

The world's first atomic bomb test, given the codename "Trinity," took place on July 16, 1945 in New Mexico, USA. The blast sent a huge mushroom cloud surging 38,000 feet into the sky

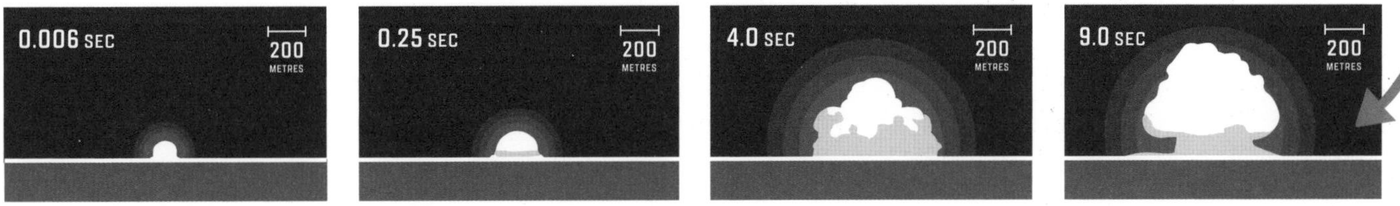

0.006 SEC
200 METRES
0.25 SEC
200 METRES
4.0 SEC
200 METRES
9.0 SEC
200 METRES

5.29am
The time the bomb went off

The heat of the blast was **10,000 times hotter** than the surface of the sun

280 miles
How far away the light of the explosion was seen

2,678°F+
The temperature of the sand on the desert floor, which melted

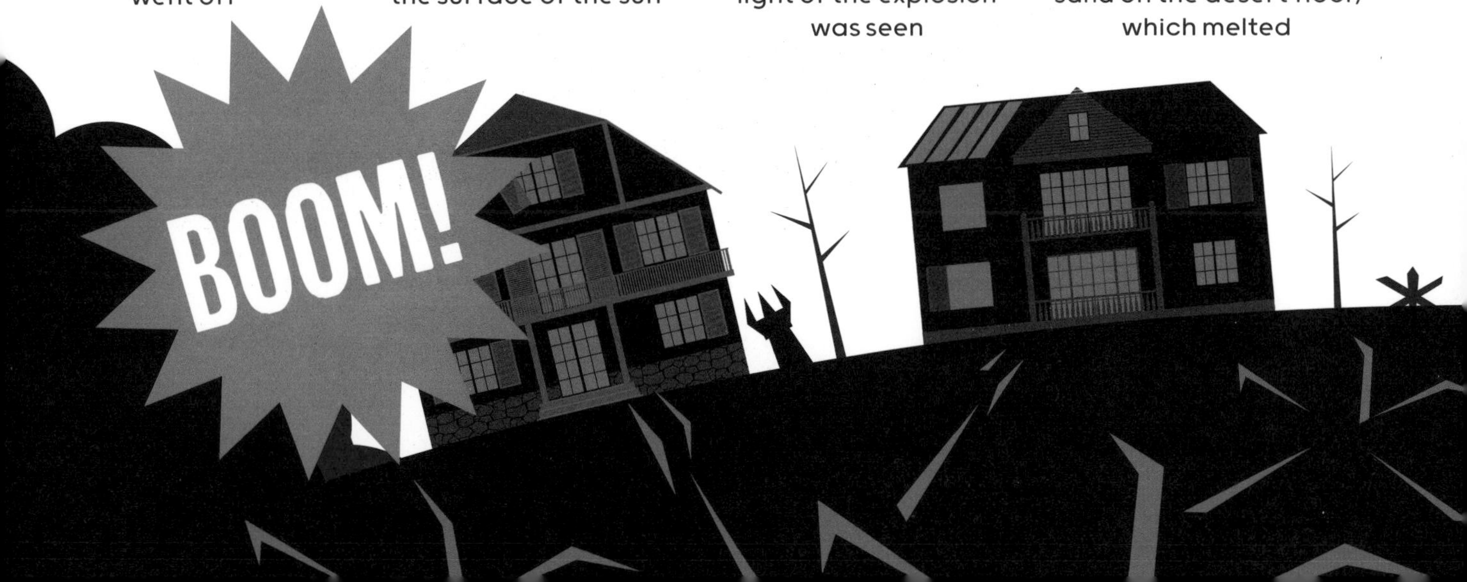

BOOM!

SUPER STAR!

Stephen spent a lot of his time at Cambridge researching black holes and he became an expert on them. He believed they held clues to how the universe began and to finding a "theory of everything."

WHAT IS A BLACK HOLE?

Black holes are the strangest and most mysterious objects in the universe. When giant stars die they explode and become super small. Because so much matter is packed into a tiny space they have incredible gravity, pulling in everything around them–even light. Black holes are invisible, but scientists know they are there because of the way they affect things around them

TIME LORD

Stephen was obsessed with the idea of time travel and once even threw a party for time travelers. The only problem was that he sent out the invitations after the event–and no one turned up! "I sat there a long time," said Stephen, "but no one came."

EVENT HORIZON

The edge of a black hole where nothing can escape once it's crossed over is called an event horizon

You are cordially invited
to a reception
for Time Travelers

Hosted by
Professor Stephen Hawking

To be held at
The University of Cambridge
Gonville & Caius College
Trinity Street
Cambridge

Location: 52° 12' 21" N, 0° 7' 4.7" E

Time: 12:00 UT 06/28/2009

No RSVP required

DID YOU KNOW?

If Stephen had a time machine he'd visit Marilyn Monroe and Italian astronomer Galileo

PHOTON SPHERE

Gravity is so stong halfway inside a black hole that it forces light to travel in circles. Because of the way the light bends, if you were standing here and looked sideways, you could see the back of your own head!

ACCRETION DISC

Many black holes are surrounded by rings of dust and gas that haven't yet fallen over the edge, called accretion discs

10 MILLION COPIES SOLD

A BRIEF HISTORY OF TIME

40 LANGUAGES

READ ALL ABOUT IT

A Brief History of Time spent four years on bestseller lists around the world and featured in the 1998 *Guinness Book of Records* as an all-time bestseller

WOO-HOO!

WHAT IF I FELL IN?

If you drove a spaceship up to the edge of a black hole, the nose of your ship (closest to the edge) would experience gravity's pull far more than the other end. This means the nose would start to accelerate more quickly than the back, stretching you and your ship out like a piece of spaghetti. Scientists call this spaghettification!

People used to think that black holes couldn't get smaller because nothing could escape their gravity. Stephen discovered that this wasn't true–he showed that some tiny particles do get free at the edge of a black hole. This stream of escaping particles is known as Hawking Radiation

HAWKING RADIATION

THE BIG BANG!

Stephen worked with another scientist called Roger Penrose to show that if you could travel to the center of a black hole you'd find something called a singularity–a tiny point packed with matter. This helped him to prove the idea that the universe we can see today began with the Big Bang.

BANG!

| 10^{32} milliseconds | 0.01 milliseconds | 0.01-200 seconds | 380,000 years |

TIME

SIZE

| Grapefruit | 0.1 trillionth present size | 1 billionth present size | 0.0009 present size |

"My goal is simple. It is a complete understanding of the universe, why it is as it is and why it exists at all"

THE BIG BANG

1 The universe we can see today starts as a very hot, very dense point. It then has an incredible growth spurt, known as inflation. In a tiny fraction of a second it expands from the size of an atom to around 4 inches–the size of a grapefruit

2 Now the universe is a hot soup of minute particles called quarks and electrons

3 The temperature cools to about a trillion degrees, and quarks stick together making protons and neutrons (the building blocks of atoms)

4 The universe is so hot, atoms can't form and light can't shine

5 Protons and neutrons finally clump together with electrons to form the first atoms

6 Gases are pulled together by gravity, and the first stars and galaxies are born

7 Galaxies collide, stars die, and the material created forms new planets and stars. The universe continues to expand. Today it contains billions of galaxies, each containing millions or billions of stars

300 million years

10 billion years

13.8 billion years

PRESENT DAY

One of Stephen's wheelchairs sold for **$363,000** at auction

TOP SPEED
8 MPH

CHEEK SENSOR

Stephen communicated by tensing a single cheek muscle. A tiny infrared sensor on his glasses saw this and sent a signal to his computer

VOICE SYNTHESIZER

Stephen's robotic voice came from a synthesizer on the back of his chair. It read out the text Stephen wrote on his computer using his cheek sensor

Wheels of FORTUNE

Stephen couldn't have lived the life he did without his incredible hi-tech wheelchair. It was made in Sweden, but companies from all over the world helped to make it work.

POWER HOUSE

The wheelchair's batteries sat under the seat, and there was a back-up battery too

BOOM BOX

A special box at the bottom of his wheelchair let Stephen plug in USBs and ramp up the volume when he wanted to

DID YOU KNOW?

In the future, scientists think wheelchairs like Stephen's will be controlled using thought alone. Sensors on the neck will detect the electrical signals your brain sends to your throat muscles when you think of a word, even if you don't actually say it out loud

20 MILES

The distance Stephen's wheelchair could travel on one charge

COMPUTER SCREEN

Stephen used the screen to write his books and talks, check his emails, and contact friends on Skype

REMOTE CONTROL

A remote built into the computer meant Stephen could turn lights and the TV on and off, and open and lock doors while he was at home

Stephen was famous for his wild wheelchair driving, and once even rode over Prince Charles's toes!

IT'S GOOD TO TALK

In 1985 Stephen caught pneumonia during a trip to Geneva and it was so serious doctors thought he might die. Stephen was flown to a hospital in Cambridge, where doctors performed a tracheotomy. They cut a hole in his neck so they could place a tube into his windpipe to help him breathe. They saved his life, but Stephen lost the ability to speak.

At first the only way Stephen could communicate was by raising his eyebrows to signal which letters he wanted as they were held up on cards. A friend of his spoke to a computer programmer in California about a special program he had made that could turn text into speech. To start with Stephen chose letters using a hand-held clicker, and when he couldn't use his thumbs anymore he used his cheek.

~~~ 6/1
Clear
Speak
j
Write
Spell

the
to
my
why
3.65~~~

INPUT

Because Stephen had little control over his muscles, he couldn't just type the words he wanted to say. Instead, an infrared switch on his glasses caught any movement in his cheek muscle

INTERFACE

Next, a cursor would move across a keyboard on his screen. When it reached the letter Stephen wanted, he'd stop it with a twitch of his cheek. Predictive text made it easier for Stephen to form words and sentences

WORDS PER MINUTE

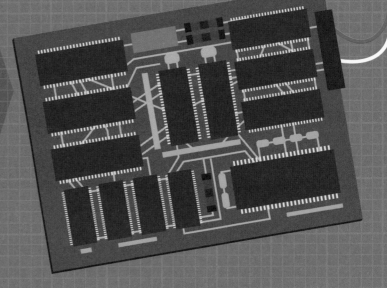

15 How fast Stephen could communicate in the early days using a hand-held clicker

1 The speed Stephen could communicate by moving his cheek muscle to express one letter at a time

MAIN MENU ~~~~ 11:40:15~~~~~
No   Maybe   Don't kno
h   g   w
y   r   t
-s   -er   -ing
Misc

what
of
can
not
PEAKING~~~~

OUTPUT

Lastly, the finished sentence was spoken out loud by a speech synthesizer. Stephen's voice was invented by American computer engineer Dennis Klatt. He made three different voices to start with, using recordings of his wife, his daughter, and himself. He called the voice based on his wife's "Beautiful Betty," his daughter's "Kit the Kid," and his own "Perfect Paul." Perfect Paul is Stephen's voice, and that's why it has a slight American accent

HAWKING

180 + PAPERS WRITTEN

15 BOOKS WRITTEN

DISABILITY
ALS

BORN
ENGLAND

BAD HABITS
MAKING BETS

2 WIVES

CHILDHOOD
LATE READER

NOBEL PRIZE?
NO

EDUCATION
PhD

AGE OF DEATH
76

FAMOUS FOR
HAWKING RADIATION, BRIEF HISTORY OF TIME

FAVORITE SUBJECTS
SCIENCE + MATH

DID YOU KNOW?

Stephen died on Albert Einstein's birthday, March 14. It's also known as Pi Day, because in month/day format it's the same as the first three digits of π: 3/14

IQ 160 +

"People who boast about their IQ are losers"

EINSTEIN

FULL NAME: ALBERT EINSTEIN

BORN
GERMANY

CHILDHOOD
LATE READER

EDUCATION
PhD

FAVORITE SUBJECTS
SCIENCE + MATH

DISABILITY
POSSIBLE AUTISM

2 WIVES

FAMOUS FOR
THEORY OF RELATIVITY, E=MC2

IQ 160+

"Imagination is more important than knowledge"

16 BOOKS WRITTEN

300 + PAPERS WRITTEN

BAD HABITS
NOT WEARING SOCKS

NOBEL PRIZE?
YES

AGE OF DEATH
76

DID YOU KNOW?

0.03% people with IQ of 160+

99.97% rest of humankind (average IQ 100)

THAT'S ENTERTAINMENT!

From *Star Trek* to *The Simpsons*, Stephen loved to make surprise appearances on TV, radio, and film. He had a brilliant sense of humor and inspired millions of people who wouldn't normally be interested in the science of the universe.

DID YOU KNOW ?

Everyone loved Stephen's sense of humor. While touring the set of *Star Trek*, he stopped next to the warp core and said:

"I'm working on that!"

STAR TREK: THE NEXT GENERATION

1993

Stephen is still the only person to have appeared as himself on the iconic TV show. He won a round of poker against Albert Einstein and Sir Isaac Newton by bluffing

THE SIMPSONS

1999

Stephen planned to steal Homer's idea for a "doughnut-shaped universe"

FUTURAMA

2008

In one episode he became a head in a jar with laser eyes

THE BIG BANG THEORY

2012

Stephen appeared on the sitcom seven times. At one point he noticed a math mistake on genius Sheldon's thesis

LITTLE BRITAIN FOR COMIC RELIEF

2015

Stephen turned into a transformer and attacked actor David Walliams

MONTY PYTHON

2015

He had a cameo appearance on their live tour, where he knocked over scientist Brian Cox then sang *The Galaxy Song*

THE HITCHHIKER'S GUIDE TO THE GALAXY

2018

He was the voice of The Guide Mark II

MUSIC

Pink Floyd used Stephen's voice on one of their songs, *Keep Talking*

FILM

Stephen was played by Benedict Cumberbatch in BBC TV drama *Hawking*, and by Eddie Redmayne in Oscar-winning movie *The Theory of Everything*

Stephen agreed to let filmmakers use his speech synthesizer for the blockbuster *The Theory of Everything*

ALL ABOARD THE

VOMIT COMET

"The Zero-G part was wonderful, and the High-G part was no problem. I could have gone on and on. Space, here I come!"

Stephen had always longed to travel in space and in 2007, aged 65, he flew aboard a special zero-gravity aircraft nicknamed the "vomit comet," which climbed and then dived through the sky to give him a taste of weightlessness.

DID YOU KNOW?

Real astronauts carry special sick bags with face wipes and Ziploc seals to use when they get the urge to hurl

COST OF TRIP
US$3,750

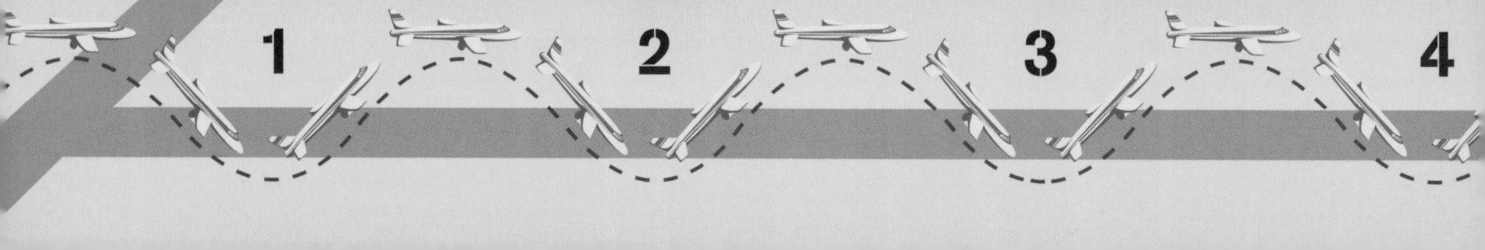
1
2
3
4

ZERO-G

The plane flies in a wave pattern of steep climbs and sharp dives. At the top of the wave, just before the plane makes a dive, passengers float weightless for around 25 seconds. During this time they can get up, jump around, and do flips, feeling what it would be like to be on a spacecraft in orbit. Although being weightless feels a bit like falling, so lots of people just flail around!

The specially modified jet belongs to space tourism company Zero Gravity Corp, which offers rides similar to those NASA uses to train astronauts

BOEING 727

1 in 3 people throw up on their first flight, hence the name "vomit comet"

2 HOUR FLIGHT

4 MINUTES ZERO-G

8 DIVES

5   6   7   8

GLOSSARY

ALS
A rare disease that stops the muscles working

ATOM
The tiny building blocks that make up everything in the universe

BIG BANG
A moment in time when the universe went from being very dense to less dense very quickly

BLACK HOLE
A place in space where gravity is so strong that even light can't escape

COSMOLOGIST
A scientist who studies the universe

COXSWAIN
The person who steers and directs the crew on a racing boat

ELECTRON
One of the particles inside an atom

GALAXY
A huge collection of dust, gas, billions of stars and their solar systems, held together by gravity

GRAVITY
An attracting force that pulls all things with mass or energy toward one another

HAWKING RADIATION
The escape of particles from a black hole

INFRARED
A type of radiation that is similar to light but has a longer wavelength, so you can't see it

MOTOR NEURONES
Nerve cells

NEUTRON
One of the particles inside an atom

PHD
A special degree awarded to people who have done advanced research in a subject

PNEUMONIA
An infection of the lungs

PROTON
One of the particles inside an atom

QUARK
A tiny particle that makes up protons and neutrons

SENSOR
A device that responds to some type of input, like light, heat, or movement

UNIVERSE
Everything that exists

VOICE SYNTHESIZER
A computer system that produces a voice similar to that of a human

ZERO-G
The state of weightlessness

Button Books

First published 2020 by Button Books, an imprint of Guild of Master Craftsman Publications Ltd, Castle Place, 166 High Street, Lewes, East Sussex, BN7 1XU, UK. Copyright in the Work © GMC Publications Ltd, 2020. ISBN 978 1 78708 103 1. Distributed by Publishers Group West in the United States. All rights reserved. No part of this publication may be reproduced, stored in a retrieval system, or transmitted in any form or by any means without the prior permission of the publisher and copyright owner. While every effort has been made to obtain permission from the copyright holders for all material used in this book, the publishers will be pleased to hear from anyone who has not been appropriately acknowledged and to make the correction in future reprints. The publishers and authors can accept no legal responsibility for any consequences arising from the application of information, advice, or instructions given in this publication. A catalog record for this book is available from the British Library. Senior Project Editor: Susie Duff. Design: Matt Carr, Jo Chapman. Illustrations: Alex Bailey, Matt Carr, Shutterstock. Color origination by GMC Reprographics. Printed and bound in China.